![CGP]

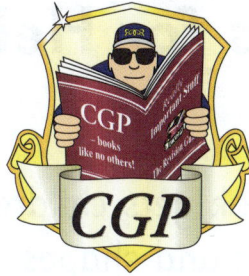

Writing
Activity Book

for ages 3-4

This CGP book is bursting with bright and colourful Writing activities for pre-school children.

It's a brilliant way to introduce the essential skills — and it's stacks of fun too!

Hints for Helpers

1) The first half of this book gets children to practise pencil control by drawing lines and shapes. In the second half of the book, they can move on to forming letters.

2) The 'Master artist' activity in the centre uses letters from the whole book — you may want to save this activity until last.

3) Children should use a pencil or their finger to trace the lines and letters in this book. Children can use their right or left hand — whichever they find easier.

4) For each letter or line, there is a dot showing where to start. When a new letter is introduced, there are arrows to follow to complete the letter.

5) You can help by reading the instructions out loud, and by sounding out the letters and words on the pages.

6) If your child finds a letter or line tricky, encourage them to try tracing it in the air or on a piece of paper with their finger. Then try again with the pencil.

7) Your child will need to learn to use the correct grip when using a pencil. They might start by holding the pencil in their fist, but they should eventually move to holding the pencil in their fingers. This is called a 'tripod' grip.

8) You may want to help your child with their writing by providing other activities that improve their finger strength, such as playing with dough.

9) Bear in mind that every nursery or school has its own handwriting style. Some schools may form letters differently to how they're written here — for example, k instead of k.

Contents

Published by CGP

Editors: Izzy Bowen, Andy Cashmore, Emma Crighton, Adam Worster

With thanks to Sharon Gulliver and Sean Walsh for the proofreading.

With thanks to Jan Greenway for the copyright research.

ISBN: 978 1 78908 606 5

Printed by Elanders Ltd, Newcastle upon Tyne. Cover and graphics used throughout the book © www.edu-clips.com Cover design concept by emc design ltd.

Text, design, layout and original illustrations © Coordination Group Publications Ltd. (CGP) 2020 All rights reserved.

Straight lines

How It Works

Straight lines don't have curves but some have bends.

Trace these lines with your finger.

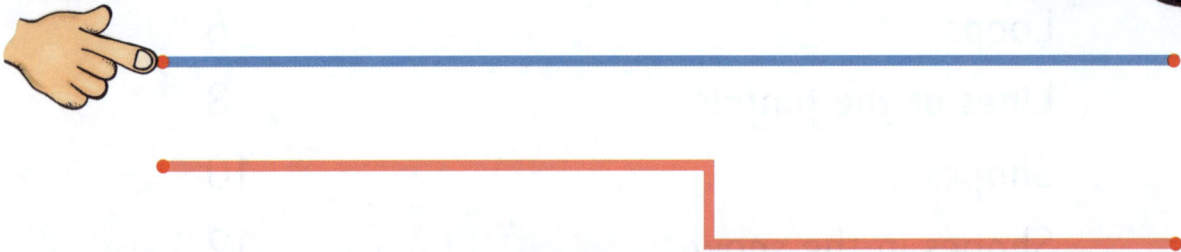

Now Try These

Draw straight lines to join the red dots.

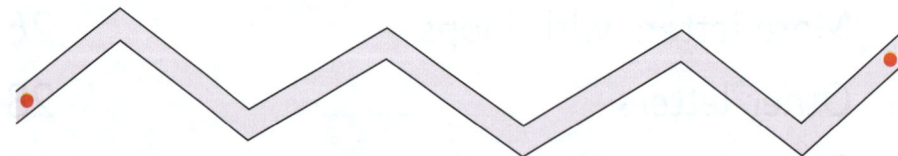

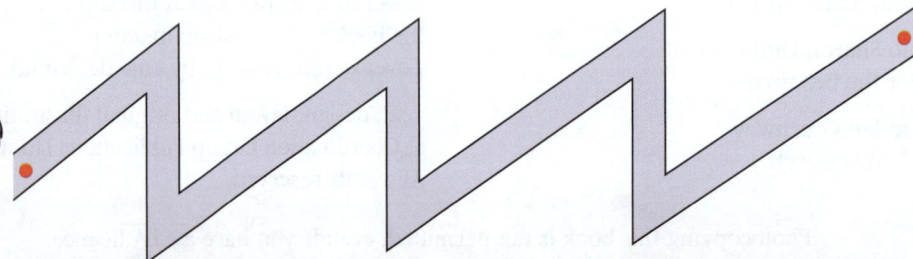

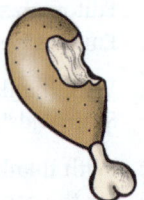

Draw a path through the maze to help Baxter find his bone.

Finish drawing the dog's kennel, then colour it in.

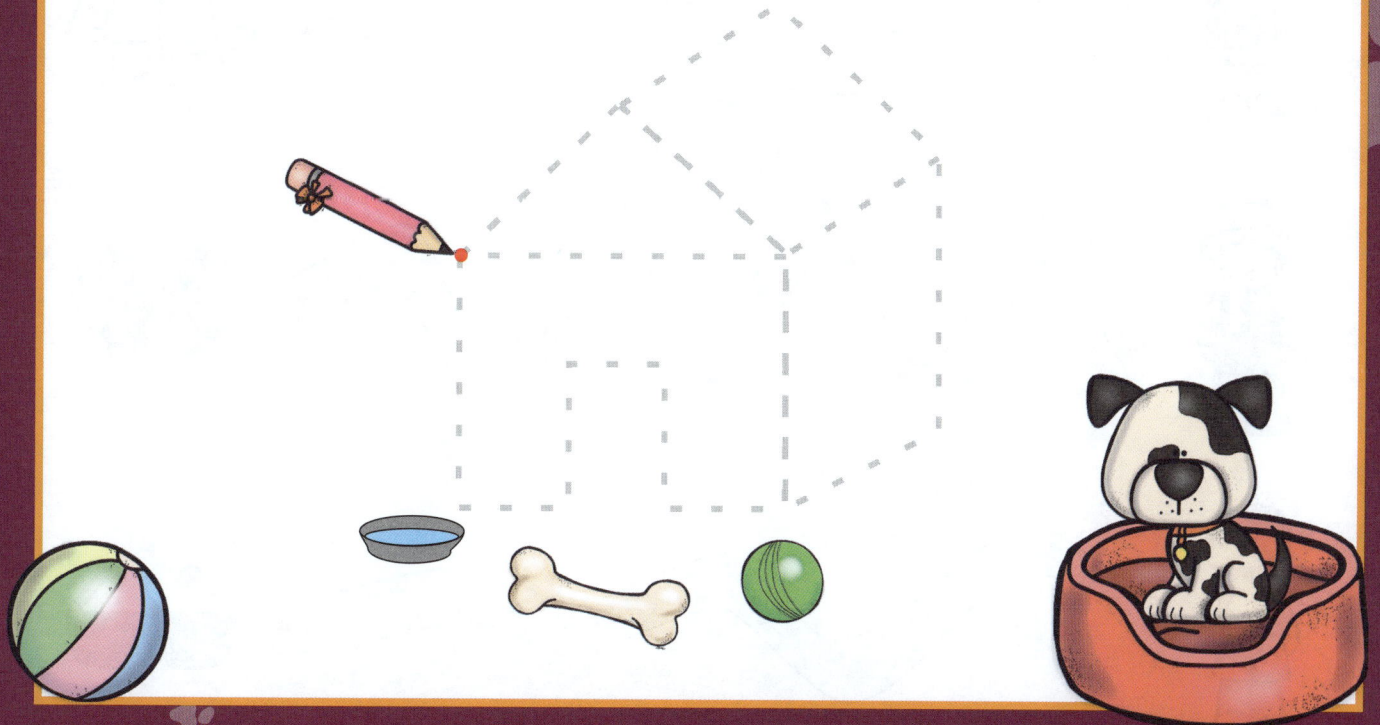

Great work — you're a straight line star! Colour the smiley face.

3

Wavy lines

Wavy lines have curves and aren't straight.

Try tracing these lines with your finger.

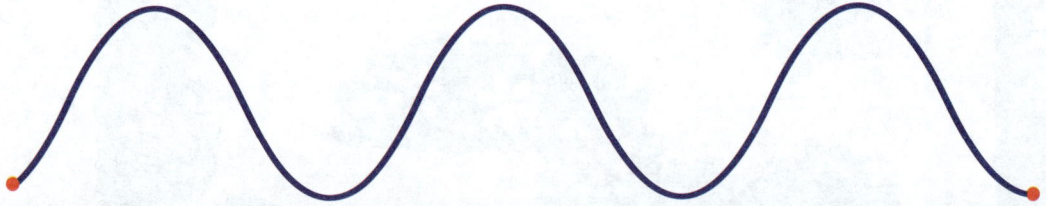

Draw wavy lines to join the red dots.

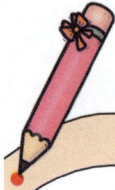

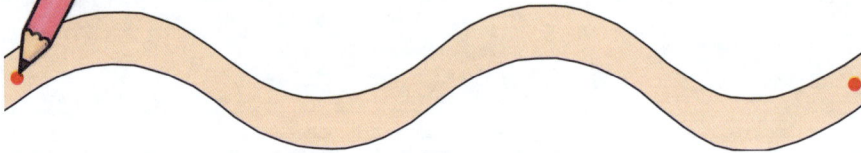

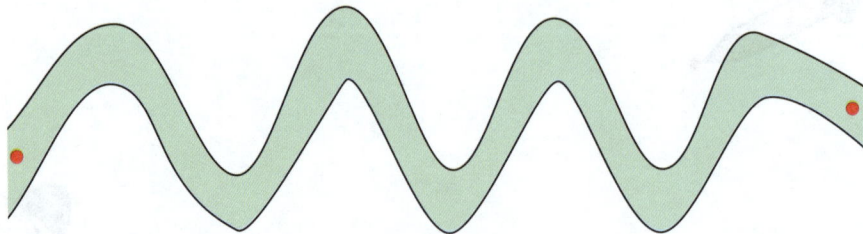

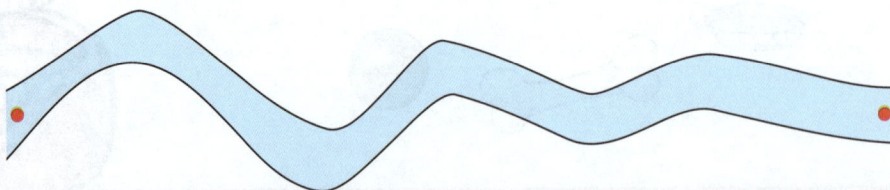

4

Draw around the clouds, then colour the picture in.

Can you draw a path from the car to the beach?

Well done for doing all of the wavy lines! Colour the smiley face.

5

How It Works

You have to go forward, then up and around, to do a loop.
Use your finger to trace the line.

Now Try These

Trace the loops behind the bugs.
Start with your pencil on the red dot.

Draw a path to help the bee find the hive.

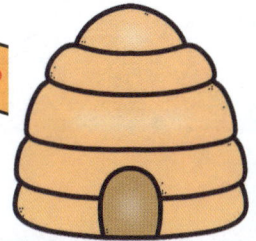

Finish drawing the butterfly, then colour it in.

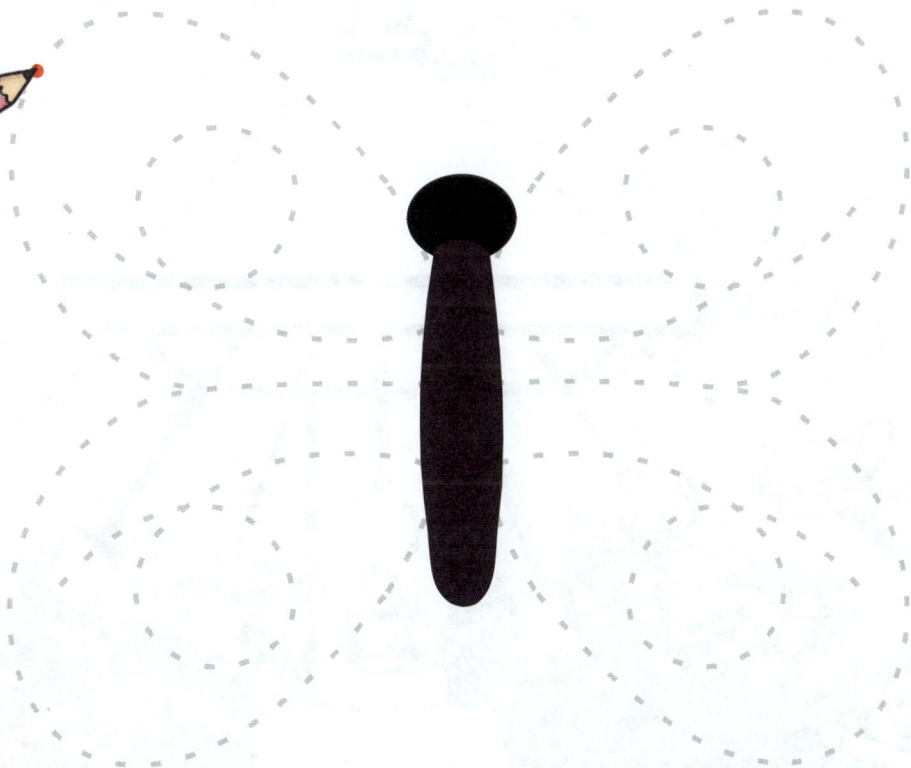

Those are some great loops! Colour the smiley face.

7

Lines at the funfair

How It Works

Here are some more lines for you to trace with your finger.

Now Try These

Draw along the dotted lines, then finish colouring the picture in.

Draw lines to show the teddies how to get around the funfair.

Draw along the dotted lines to make a rollercoaster.

Well done — you're a line superstar! Colour the smiley face.

How It Works

Can you trace these shapes with your finger?

 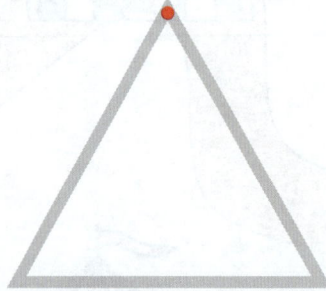 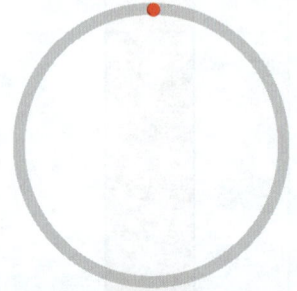

Now Try These

Practise drawing the shapes below.

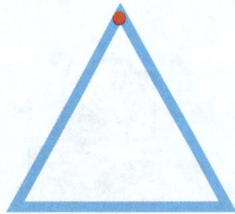 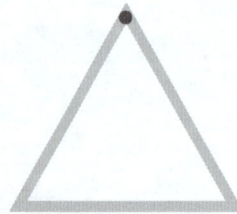 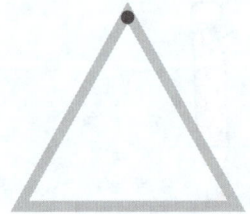

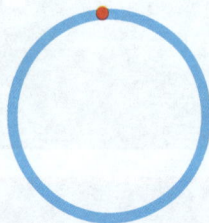 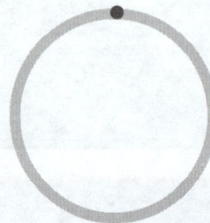 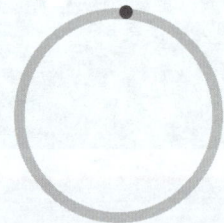

Can you help Harry the Hero catch the villain?
Draw the stepping stones to help Harry cross the river.

Draw around the dotted lines,
then finish colouring the picture.

BANK

You've mastered these shapes! Colour the smiley face.

11

How It Works

Here are some more shapes. Trace them with your finger.

Now Try These

Draw around the dotted lines, then finish colouring in the picture.

Draw around the dotted lines to finish this snowy scene.

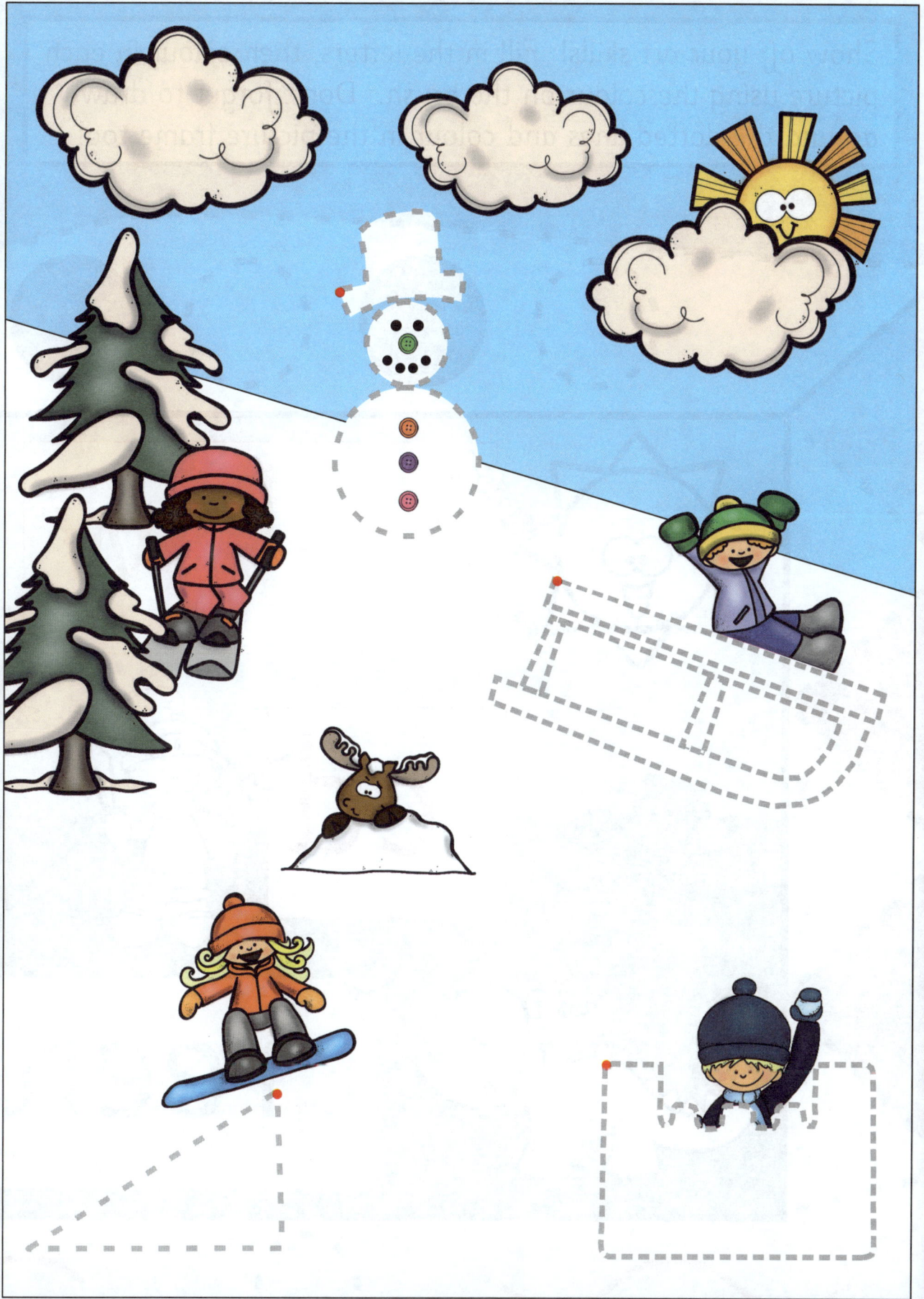

Good job — you're cool with shapes! Colour the smiley face.

13

Master artist

Show off your art skills! Fill in the letters, then colour in each picture using the colour on the brush. Don't forget to draw around the dotted lines and colour in the picture frame too!

yellow

red

green

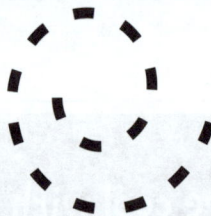

Put your name here!

This picture was made by:

_____

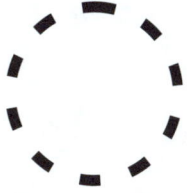  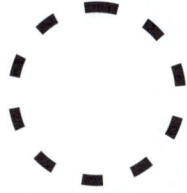 

orange

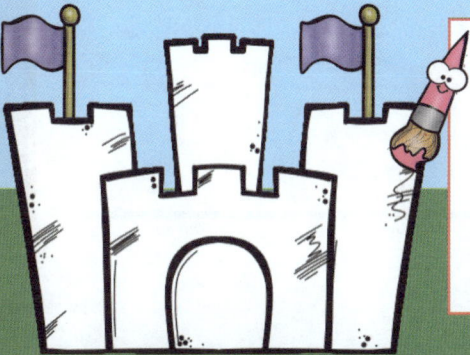

pink

blue

Round letters

How It Works

These letters all start with a round shape.
Trace the letters with your finger by following the arrows.

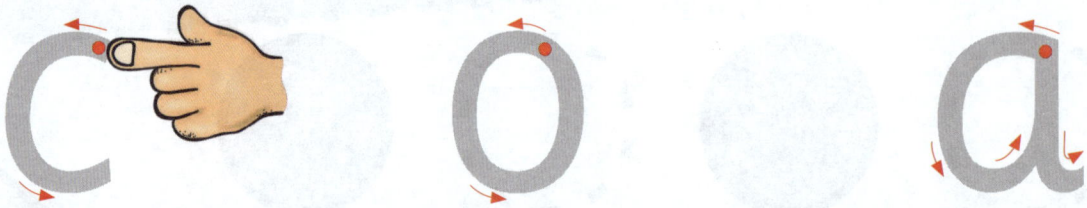

c   o   o   a

Now Try These

Practise writing the letters below.

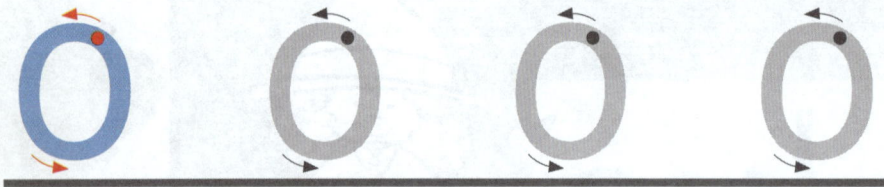

c c c c

o o o o

a a a a

Can you write these letters?

Fill in the missing letters, then colour the robot in.

and

cog

can

Great job — you can write round letters! Colour the smiley face.

17

Letters with straight lines

How It Works

These letters have a straight line. Trace the letters with your finger.

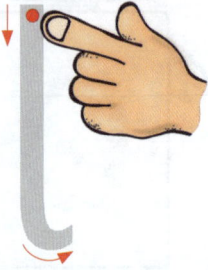

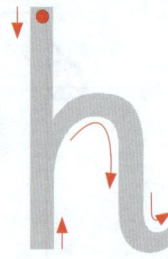

l t h k

Now Try These

Practise writing the letters below, then colour the hippo in.

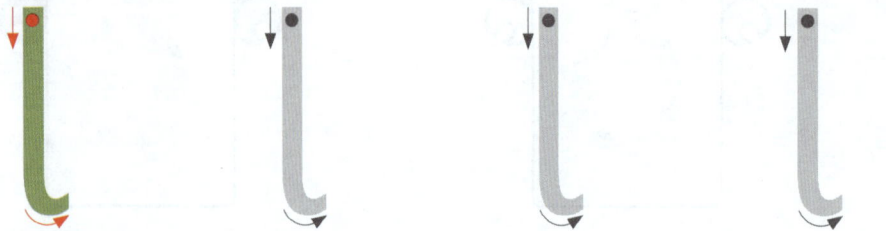

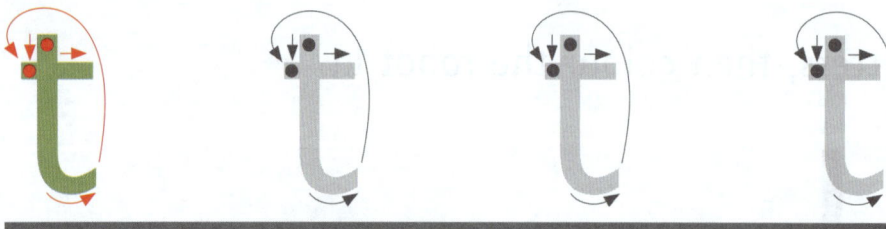

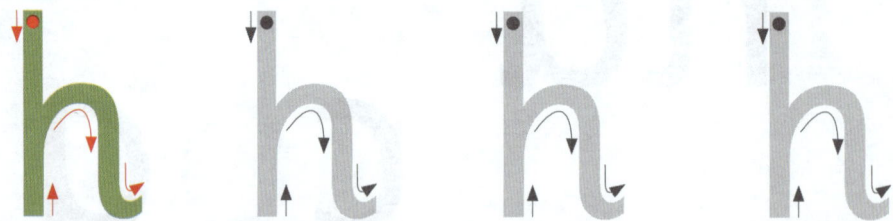

l l l l

t t t t

h h h h

k k k k

Can you write these letters?

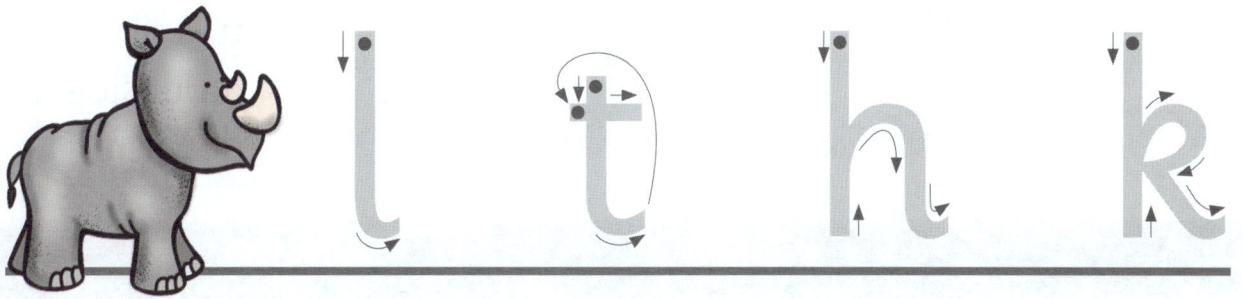

l t h k

l t h k

Fill in the missing letters.

top

leg hog

Well done — you're all lined up! Colour the smiley face.

19

Letters that go up and over

These letters all go up and over. Follow the red arrows and trace these letters with your finger.

r n m u

The letter **u** is like an upside down **n**.

Now Try These

Practise writing the letters below.

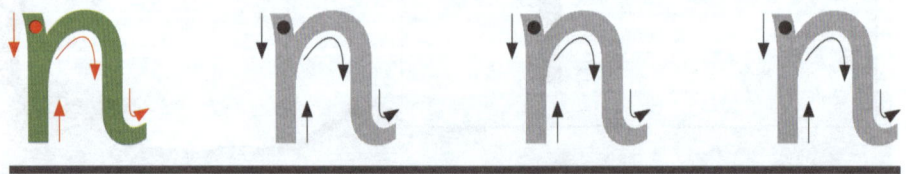

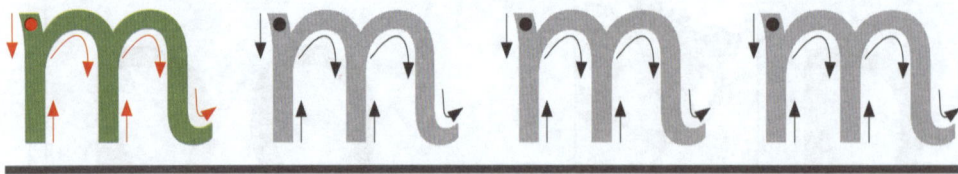

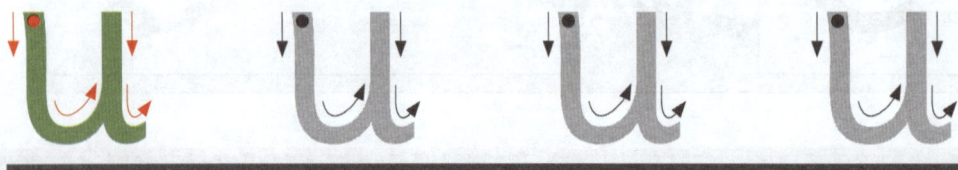

r r r r

n n n n n

m m m m

u u u u

Can you write these letters?

Fill in the missing letters, then colour the cat in.

nap   rat

mat

You've mastered these letters! Colour the smiley face.

21

Letters with dots

These two letters both have dots above them.
Follow the red arrows and trace these letters with your finger.

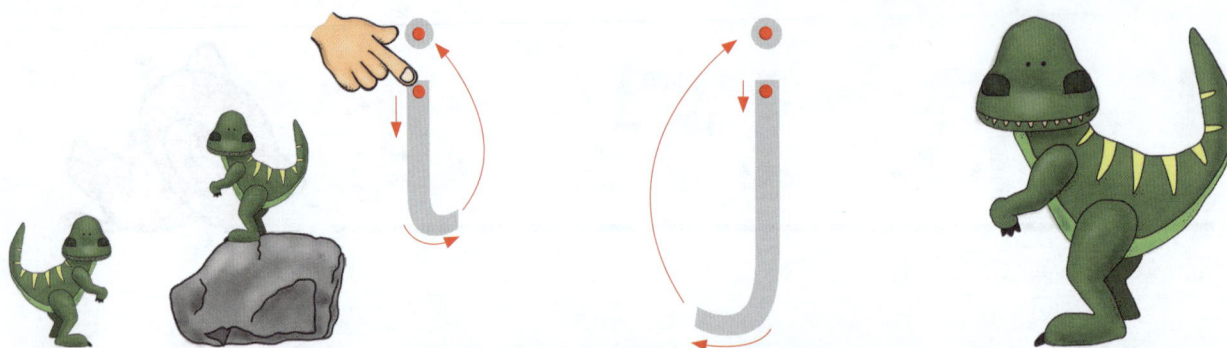

Now Try These

Practise writing the letters below.

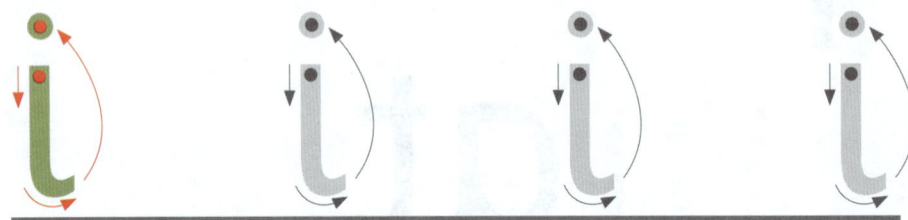

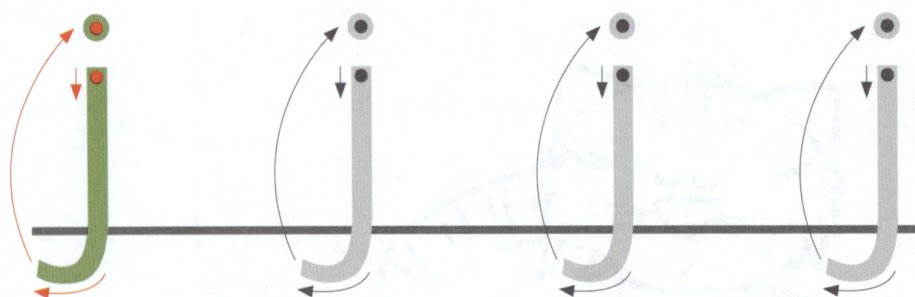

Can you write these letters?

Fill in the missing letters, then draw a circle
around the biggest dinosaur below.

big   jog

Great stuff — you're a dot expert! Colour the smiley face.

23

Letters with loops

These letters have a straight line and then a loop. Try tracing them with your finger. Start at the red dots and follow the arrows.

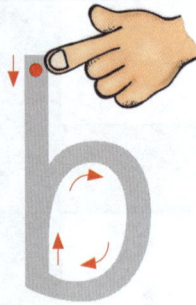

Now Try These

Practise writing the letters below.

24

Can you write these letters?

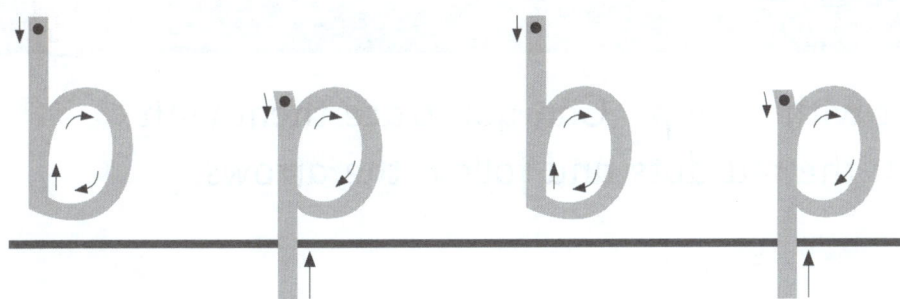

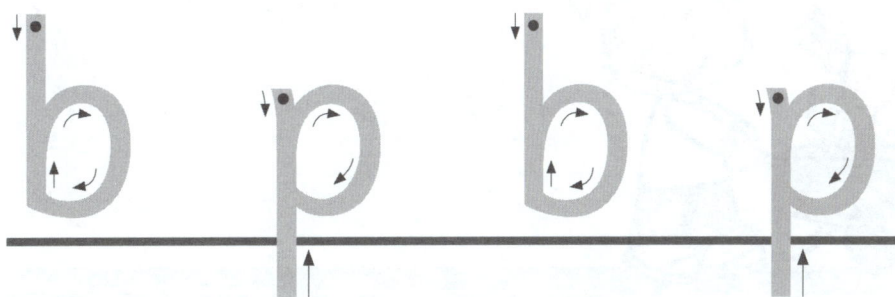

b p b p b p

b p b p b p

Fill in the missing letters.

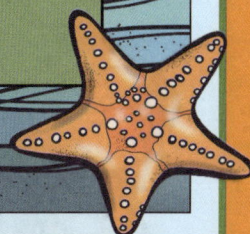

bag pit

You've finished these letters – great job! Colour the smiley face.

25

More letters with loops

How It Works

These letters all start with a loop. Can you trace them with your finger? Start at the red dots and follow the arrows.

d g q

Now Try These

Practise writing the letters below.

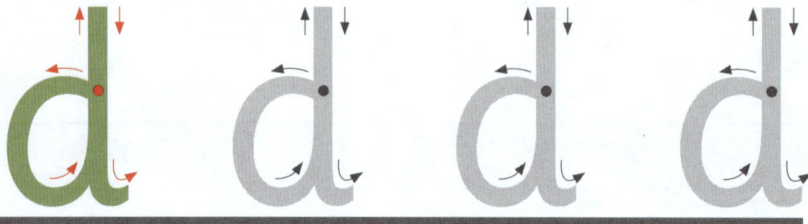

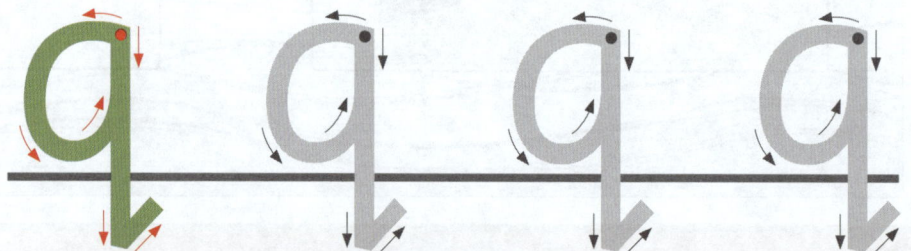

d d d d d

g g g g g

q q q q q

26

Can you write the letters on the T-shirts?

Fill in the missing letters, then colour the ladybird in.

dig   bug

You've mastered loopy letters! Colour the smiley face.

27

Other letters

Trace the letters with your finger by following the arrows.

e s f y

Practise writing the letters below.

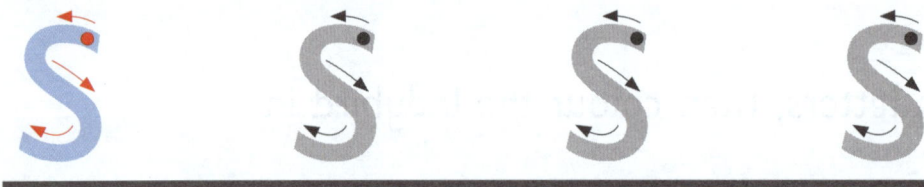

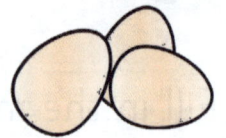

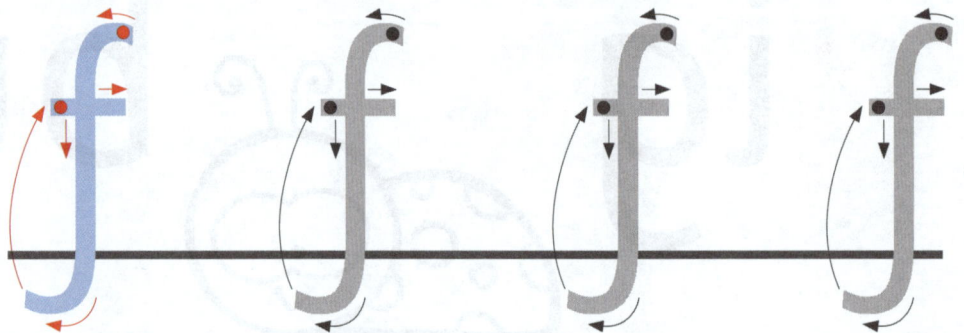

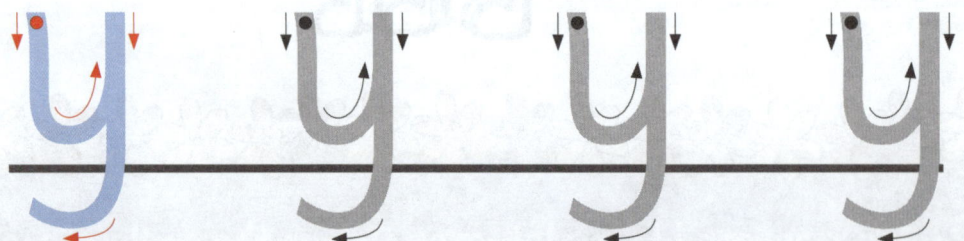

e e e e

s s s s

f f f f

y y y y

Can you write these letters?

e s f y

e s f y

Fill in the missing letters.

egg

fun

sit

You're growing into a great writer! Colour the smiley face.

29

Zigzags and crosses

How It Works

These letters use zigzags and crosses.
Trace the letters with your finger by following the arrows.

V W X Z

You'll need to lift your pencil off the page to cross the **x**.

Now Try These

Practise writing the letters below.

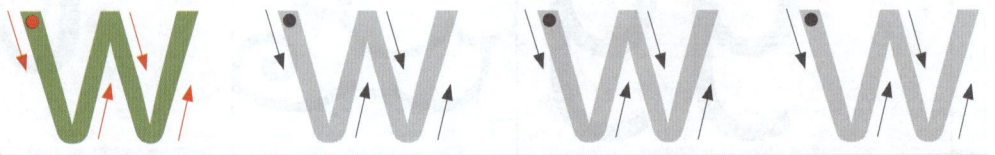

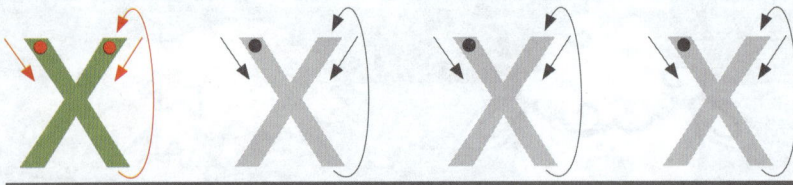

V V V V

W W W W W

X X X X X

Z Z Z Z Z

Cross those letters off your to-do list! Colour the smiley face.

30

EPFEH01